TRY THIS ONE... TOO

IDEAS FOR YOUTH GROUPS

Edited by Lee Sparks

Illustrations by Alan Wilkes
and Rand Kruback

GROUP BOOKS

P.O. Box 481
Loveland, CO 80539

Selected from the regular feature "Try This One"
in GROUP, the magazine for Christian youth groups.

TRY THIS ONE... TOO

Copyright © 1982 by Thom Schultz Publications, Inc.

Library of Congress Catalog No. 82-081331

ISBN 0-936664-05-3

CONTENTS

Introduction 5

Fun 'n Games 7

Group Growth Goodies 45

Fun Fund Raisers 63

Note 79

INTRODUCTION

Since GROUP Magazine appeared in 1974, the feature "Try This One" has enjoyed enormous popularity. We believe this popularity stems from the unquenchable thirst for innovative ideas for all kinds of youth group activities. This group of 100 "Try This One" ideas helps satisfy that thirst.

Try This One . . . Too is the third collection of ideas from "Try This One" in GROUP. The ideas in this volume were born out of a creative desire to help young people grow closer to one another, and closer to God. The authors are leaders and members of Christian youth groups all over the country. Their ideas were tested in local church settings . . . and found successful.

Try This One . . . Too is a shopping center of ideas—some zany, some serious, some profitable. The "Fun 'n Games" section gives ideas for fun crowd breakers, games, parties and special events. The ideas in the "Group Growth Goodies" section help members grow in Christ, both as individuals and as a group. The "Fun Fund Raisers" section offers new profit-making ventures that meet persons' needs.

Feel free to adapt these ideas. Enlarge them, combine them, enjoy them. Then let your creative genius free to create new ideas—and send them to us. See the note on page 79 for details.

FUN 'N GAMES

GIZMO GUESS

Here's a game that taps the creativity of your members.

Collect about a dozen strange objects—gadgets, gizmos, tools, anything that would be totally unfamiliar to your group. Number them consecutively and let your group play "dictionary."

Each member concocts a name and function for item No. 1 and writes it on a 3x5 card. Encourage creative and ridiculous descriptions. A leader collects and shuffles the cards, including an additional card that describes what the object truly is.

All cards are then read aloud. Points are awarded to each person who guesses the right card. When someone guesses a phony description, points go to the writer of the bogus card.

Repeat this procedure for item No. 2, and so on.

The person with the most points at the end is the winner.

—Joseph E. Srebro, Peoria, Illinois

SQUIRT HUNT

Here's a wet and wild game.

Blindfold two guys or girls and put them at opposite ends of the room with their teams. Inform the teams that the only things they can say are directions like right-left, forward-back, up-down. Place a squirt gun somewhere in the room and let the blindfolded kids try to find it.

It is hilarious watching them try to listen to their team shouting directions at the same time the other team is shouting. Award points for the first to find the gun.

You may also award points to the person who doesn't find it if he/she can touch the "finder" before being squirted.

—Gary Sumner, El Centro, California

PANTOMIME INITIATION

Here's a fun initiation ceremony for new members in your group.

Instruct the new members to act out a really strange action, such as a piece of chewing gum being taken out of the wrapper and popped into someone's mouth. Everything must be portrayed.

So, for example, someone would be the stick of gum, another would be the wrapper, and somebody else would be the mouth.

Other action ideas: flying a kite, a bowl of ice cream on a hot day, an automobile dashboard (with all the gauges), a typewriter, and a brush involved in house-painting.

Get ready for a lot of laughs.

—Kelly J. Cox, Bryan, Ohio

9

PEOPLE HUNT

Here's an adventuresome way for your group to mix with new members.

The people hunt takes place in a busy airport, shopping mall, or any other large place where many people roam.

There are two types of people in a people hunt—the "hunted" and the "hunters." The hunters should outnumber the hunted.

One of your adult leaders meets with the hunted (new members) at the airport. The hunted then have their pictures taken in the photo booth (or they may bring along a photo of themselves). They may disguise themselves a little—with sunglasses, a hat, or whatever. Then the hunted spread out. Bathrooms are off limits.

About a half hour after the hunted arrive, the hunters should come as a group to the airport. They are divided into groups of three and given a photo of the person to be hunted. When a team finds a hunted person, they exchange a coded message. It might be: "Why didn't they play cards on the ark?" "Because Noah was sitting on the deck."

Then the hunter group finds another group of hunters and trades photos. The hunted keep moving around to keep the hunters busy.

Allow 45 minutes for the hunt. Then everyone meets at a pre-arranged spot. Go out for pie and get to know the people you hunted.

This activity would also work well for an entire youth group to hunt another youth group.

—Cathy Skogen, Minneapolis, Minnesota

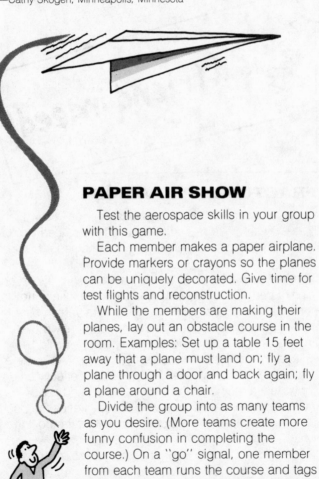

PAPER AIR SHOW

Test the aerospace skills in your group with this game.

Each member makes a paper airplane. Provide markers or crayons so the planes can be uniquely decorated. Give time for test flights and reconstruction.

While the members are making their planes, lay out an obstacle course in the room. Examples: Set up a table 15 feet away that a plane must land on; fly a plane through a door and back again; fly a plane around a chair.

Divide the group into as many teams as you desire. (More teams create more funny confusion in completing the course.) On a "go" signal, one member from each team runs the course and tags the next team member, who then runs the course. The first team to finish wins.

—Gary Hunziker, Chehalis, Washington

11

FRACTURED PROVERBS

This is a variation of the "famous couples" crowd breaker where names of famous pairs are placed in separate bowls and each person selects a name for his/her match.

In this game, famous proverbs are written or typed on slips of paper and then cut in half, but the idea is **not** to combine the original parts. On the contrary, members should be encouraged to create their own new proverbs. For example: "A watched pot never boils" would be split down the middle as would the saying, "An apple a day keeps the doctor away." It would be perfectly acceptable if a member who chose "A watched pot" matched up with a member who chose "keeps the doctor away" to make: "A watched pot keeps the doctor away."

There are no wrong or right combinations, only new ones. Prizes may be awarded for the most original proverb. Here is a list of 30 to start you off for an event for 60 people.

—Ann Lee Segal, Albuquerque, New Mexico

12

Silence is golden.

One good turn deserves another.

When in Rome do as the Romans do.

All that glitters is not gold.

The early bird catches the worm.

Birds of a feather flock together.

He who laughs last laughs best.

You can't have your cake and eat it too.

It takes two to make a quarrel.

People who live in glass houses shouldn't throw stones.

Two wrongs don't make a right.

A stitch in time saves nine.

A barking dog never bites.

A fool and his money are soon parted.

Every cloud has a silver lining.

It takes a thief to catch a thief.

All good things must come to an end.

A penny saved is a penny earned.

Honesty is the best policy.

Absence makes the heart grow fonder.

A watched pot never boils.

A rolling stone gathers no moss.

Rome wasn't built in a day.

An apple a day keeps the doctor away.

Brevity is the soul of wit.

Curiosity killed the cat.

Health is better than wealth.

A friend in need is a friend indeed.

Variety is the spice of life.

Necessity is the mother of invention.

HUNT AND CLUCK

Here's a game that's a little weird, but promises lots of laughs.

Before the group arrives, hide candy corn throughout the room or outdoor area.

Divide into two or more teams. Each team must choose a captain who will serve as a "rooster." All other team members are "hens."

On a "go" signal, all hens spread out to search for candy corn. When they find a piece of corn they are to cluck like a chicken to draw the attention of their rooster. The rooster is the only one who may pick up the corn from its hiding place. To make sure the hens do not pick up the corn, they must hold their hands behind their backs to represent wings of a chicken.

If hens from two different teams discover the same piece of corn, the rooster who arrives on the scene first gets the corn.

A rooster may pick up corn only at spots identified by his own clucking team members.

The team with the most corn is the winner.

—Brad Hogan, Elyria, Ohio

TWO-IN-A-TUBE RACE

This crazy relay is as much fun to watch as it is to play. All you need is a large box of penny balloons and several clean inner tubes.

Divide your group into two or more equal teams. In each team, pair up. Line the teams up behind a start/finish line. Place piles of balloons 50 feet or more from that line—one pile for each team. Make sure you have enough balloons in each pile (one for each team member).

The object—each pair runs to the pile of balloons, each runner picks up a balloon, blows it up, and pops it with his foot before returning to tag the next pair on the team. There is, however, a catch.

Now roll in the inner tubes. Each pair must stand, back-to-back and place their inner tube around both of them at waist height. With one member running forward and the other backward, the pair runs to the balloons. Each person must bend down, pick up a balloon, blow it up and break it with his foot while his partner is doing likewise. The inner tube must stay at waist height at all times.

After both balloons are popped the pair is allowed to run back to their team to tag the next pair of runners. The first team to get all its members back across the start/finish line is declared the winning team.

For added variety, use two inner tubes per pair instead of just one.

—Mark Kaat, Sheboygan, Wisconsin

WATER BALLOON BURGLARS

This is an outdoor, summer game that is lots of fun.

First, divide your group into two even teams. In a large grassy area, set up two tables—about 50 to 100 feet apart, and turn them on their sides. The tables' surfaces should face each other so that they make a barricade for people to hide behind. Get a bag of balloons —round ones are the best—and fill them all tightly with water. Put an equal number (15 or 20) water balloons behind each table.

Choose two members from each team to be the ''guards'' of their barricades. Blindfold everyone except the guards. All the blindfolded members of each team will stand behind their barricades until the signal to go is given. The two guards of each barricade will stand about two feet in front of their tables.

The object of the game is for team members to try to steal the other team's water balloons and put them behind their own barricade.

16

The four guards are not allowed to touch the water balloons with their hands, but they may hinder the other team from reaching its goal by leading the blind in the wrong direction. The guards are also there to prevent either of the teams from knocking heads or running into anything else.

At the end of seven minutes, whichever team has the greatest number of unbroken water balloons behind its table wins.

Make sure you come prepared to get slightly wet!

Hint: If you're having trouble getting at the other team's balloons because a guard is keeping you out, try ganging up on him. Everyone jump on him—some of you hold him down while the rest of you steal the stashed balloons.

—Dave Silvey, Alexandria, Pennsylvania

BENT OUT OF SHAPE

You can really get twisted and bent out of shape with this game.

The group is divided into three equal lines facing a caller. The caller begins by saying, "All those who. . . (i.e. didn't take a bath today, use Preparation H, own a stereo, etc.) grab the left knee of the person in front of you." The leader asks another "all those who . . ." question, then gives a command such as, "grab the right elbow of the person to your left." Continue until everyone is tied in knots.

—Dennis and Susan Henn, Wenatchee, Washington

17

PROJECT-A-SKIT

This is a modern version of the old shadow game.

Use an overhead projector as a light source to silhouette your image onto a white sheet suspended between your audience and the actors. Any item or drawing that is put on the viewing glass of the projector will accompany the shadows cast by the performers.

Here's a sample of the wild effects you can produce. Stand two people, one behind the other, so that they cast a single person shadow on the sheet. Now place a small knife blade on the projector and move it in a sawing motion from the top to the bottom of the people shadow. When completed, have the two actors fall to opposite sides to end this dramatic visual.

Experiment with the projector using images such as two hands closing together, a shoe, pencils, paper cutout monsters, or wherever your imagination leads.

Divide into teams and create fun mini-dramas. Award a prize to the best presentation.

Be prepared for shadow marathons. Some people can't quit!

—Dick Fischer, Loveland, Colorado

FLIPPER/FLOPPER

Try this simple game for some crazy fun.

Divide your group into pairs. One person is the "flipper," the other the "flopper." Form a circle about 30 feet in diameter. An object or prize is in the middle of the circle. Be sure each team is an equal distance from the center.

The goal is to reach the center first. On a "go" signal, the flipper (who stands behind the flopper) flips a coin. If

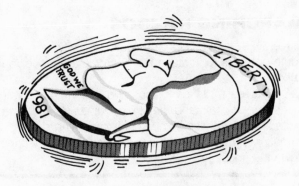

heads come up, the flopper takes two steps forward. If tails come up, the flopper must take one step back. Steps consist of "heel to toe" steps only.

Things get crowded toward the center—and the fun really increases.

—Gary Hunziker, Chehalis, Washington

KISS-THE-PIG CONTEST

Need a new and different incentive to build attendance in your group? Try pig kissing.

A Young Life club in Rochester, New York, challenged the sophomores, juniors and seniors to an attendance contest. The class bringing the highest number of new kids to meetings over a three-week period was the winner. Representatives from the losing two classes were required to kiss a live pig during a club meeting.

Jim Kirkley, area Young Life director, brought a 40-pound porker to the climactic meeting. "Oh, it was gross," he said. "The pig stunk to high heaven." But the losers in the contest were good sports—they each landed a juicy smack on the snout of the special guest of honor.

MARCHING KAZOOS

Here's a great group participation activity for a whole youth group or for a stage performance at a large youth rally.

Give at least 20 kids kazoos and marching band uniforms or party hats and matching clothes (i.e., jeans and white shirts). Practice some simple marching drills and formations. (Finishing with a giant kick line really brings down the house.)

Perform this with recorded march music such as "Stars and Stripes Forever." Play the music just loud enough to be heard along with the kazoos.

This was especially effective at a special meeting we held with a football theme. Between four quarters of different activities we had this great half-time show. The response was terrific.

—Janice Parylak, Deer Park, New York

CHURCH CLUES

This is a fun game in which your members must think to keep moving from place to place in the church building.

The group meets at a specific place in the building at a set time. The leader explains the game and reveals the first clue of the meeting's journey.

At each place conduct part of the meeting. For example, a clue may lead to a bulletin board where members find instructions to make announcements. After the announcements, a clue leads the group to the sanctuary for some singing. A clue in the last song leads them to the kitchen for refreshments. Finally a clue points them toward a meeting room for devotions.

The leader's role is to encourage participation and offer bits of help to solve clues. "Church Clues" adds life and a touch of mystery to meetings.

—Richard Davis, Lewisville, Texas

GREAT SACK LUNCH

Have some big eaters in your group? Here's a stunt just for them.

Fill five lunch bags with the following items. Put a banana in the first bag; two pickles in the second bag; three marshmallows in the third bag; four Ritz crackers in the fourth bag; and a sardine in the fifth bag. Make up at least two sets of these bags. (You'll need a set for each hungry eater.)

Ask for volunteer big eaters to come to the front. Explain that the object of this game is to eat the contents of each sack, in succession. The eaters start at one end of the room, run to the other end, pick up a sack, run back to a spot near the rest of the group, open the sack and eat the contents. The eater then throws the sack over his shoulder and dashes for the next sack.

You can imagine the surprise (and laughs) when the eaters discover the contents of the last sack. In our group, two out of three eaters were able to complete the race—sardine and all.

—Dick Copeland, Lewisville, Texas

DAFFY DATA

When your group acquires some new members, it is often helpful to get some basic information on each individual—name, address, interests, etc. Instead of boring questionnaires, here's a fun way to get the information.

As each person arrives, give him or her a piece of paper, with one of two numbers on it. After everyone has come, divide into two teams, using the numbers on the papers. Explain that the teams will be competing, and the team scoring the most points will win. To get points, each person must answer, in writing, some questions.

Questions should include "What is your full name?" and "What is your telephone number?" as well as goofy questions such as "Have you ever touched a camel?" Decide beforehand (but don't announce) what answers to give points for, such as 10 points for the person born closest to June 20, or for the team with the most members who dislike cauliflower. The less logic used in deciding points, the better and funnier. Have the final question worth a lot, so that either team could still have a chance. Maybe this will be the chance for the perpetual loser to become the hero by being the only one to remember the name of Mr. Ed's owner.

After the contest, collect the papers, and you will have painlessly gathered all the necessary information, plus a whole lot more. And you'll all get a little better acquainted in the process.

—Wayne Pauluk, Minneapolis, Minnesota

JAIL HOUSE BLUES

"Jail House Blues" is a great activity to attract new members and excite the regulars.

Everyone arrives dressed in "rough criminal" cos-

tumes. As each arrives, take Polaroid-type "mug shots" with criminal numbers. Also take group shots in front of a height-marked police line-up background.

After photos, take thumb prints. Occasionally say something like, "This one looks like the type who would cut off her thumbs! We better print all her fingers (or toes!)." Interrogate everyone under a hot light, writing down name, address, phone, school, hobbies and other information.

After booking the crooks, hold a kangaroo court, where each member receives sentencing for some "dastardly" crime. Then send the criminals to jail for "bread and water" (refreshments).

This is a great time to pass out calendars of youth activities for the coming year or quarter. You may also want to come together for a devotion on Paul's imprisonment. Check your local public library for a short Keystone Cops flick.

We used "Jail House Blues" as a kick-off program for our fall meetings. Retreats would also be a good setting for the activity. However used, "Jail House Blues" builds relationships and provides a photo and lots of information on each group member and visitor.

—Tommy Baker and Doug Newhouse, Florence, Kentucky

CHRISTMAS CARD PUZZLER

Sometimes it's hard deciding how to break a group into teams. Do it with old Christmas cards. Here's how.

Select several cards that are quite different from one another. Cut the front panel off the cards. Now cut each of the panels into several puzzle pieces (the number of pieces per card will determine the number of people per team).

Put all pieces into one bag. As your members arrive allow each person to select one piece from the bag. Then, at a given signal, everyone tries to find the other people who'll help complete his/her puzzle card. If you wish, you can run this as a contest. The first team to complete a puzzle is the winner.

When all cards are completed, you have your teams for the evening.

—Ron Bodager, Newnan, Georgia

THE KILLER

How subtle can you be? Try this one.

Have your group sit in a circle with a deck of cards. Deal out all of the cards. The person who receives the ace of spades is "The Killer." This person should not let anyone know that he/she holds the ace of spades.

Once the cards are all distributed, members start looking at one another. "The Killer" will wink at somebody. The person who's winked at silently counts to ten and says, "I'm dead," and falls out.

It's up to the group to identify "The Killer" before it's too late.

If your church objects to cards, the game can easily be played with 3x5 cards—all blank except for one that has a small X on it.

—Phil Sexton, Jacksonville, Florida

CLOSE-UP SOUNDS

It can be just as challenging—and almost as much fun—preparing to play "Close-Up Sounds" as it is actually playing it.

You'll need a tape recorder and any ordinary household items that happen to be lying around. Take different items and make sounds with them into the tape recorder—close up, right next to the mike. For instance, blow into the mike. It will sound like a tremendous explosion. Click a pen, rustle the pages of a book, strum the teeth of a comb. Use your imagination!

The group then tries to identify each sound. When you've gone through all the sounds and played them back to everyone's satisfaction, one or two people go off into another room to conjure up their own batch of sounds. And so on.

You can be formal if you like, with everyone writing down their guesses and keeping score. You could divide into teams. But it's really more fun to play with everyone shouting out their own impressions, like in charades.

—Judy Carney, Louisville, Kentucky

I HAVE NEVER . . .

For this crowdbreaker, give everyone 30 pieces of string. One person begins by saying, "I have never . . . (something he/she has never done)." Everyone who has done what the speaker has never done gives the speaker a piece of string. If no one in the circle has done it, the speaker gives each player a piece of string. There's no time limit.

The winner is the one with the greatest number of pieces of string. The game's strategy is to say something you've never done that you think many others have done. Example: "I have never downhill skied." Since many in my group have downhill skied, I would get lots of string pieces.

—Karen Hartman, Prince George, British Columbia

BUBBLE GUM MOBILE

If you're looking for something a little weird, try making a bubble gum mobile. This project has no socially redeeming value other than being a lot of fun. Plus, it will give your group a simple project to work on together, and you can offer your pastor a gift that'll leave him speechless.

Depending on the size of your group and its gum chewing habits, you'll need one or two clothes hangers, strong string (cotton is better than nylon) and lots of chewy, sticky, colorful bubble gum. (Regular chewing gum is smaller, not as workable as bubble gum, and doesn't have the rich variety of colors. Besides, worn-out bubbles make interesting designs for mobiles.)

The process is simple: Tie different lengths of string to the empty clothes hanger and attach it to the ceiling so it hangs just above eye level. Then, for six weeks or so, have a formal time in each meeting for an "add-to-the-mobile" session. You'll have fun trying different ways of attaching the gum to the string to make interesting and classy designs. It won't take long for some people to find interesting ways of grossing out the others in your group who have weak stomachs.

Once you've completed your creation, present it to your minister for prominent display. Give him permission to chew any of the gum he finds tempting.

BLIND PRINCE SHOE GRAB

Try this funny game in your group.

Choose five guys and five girls (or any equal number). The girls are the Cinderellas and the guys are the princes. The Cinderellas sit in chairs. Each prince kneels in front of his lady and removes her shoes. Each Cinderella is then given a blindfold, which she puts on her prince.

Now a leader takes all the shoes and puts them in a line, all mixed up, behind the princes. When the leader gives a signal, each Cinderella tries to direct her prince to where her shoes are located. She must stay seated at all times.

Get ready for a lot of yelling and fun confusion.

The first prince to find the right shoes and put them on his Cinderella wins. Actually, both the prince and the Cinderella are winners.

—Stacey Hiatt, Sugar Grove, Ohio

SPAGHETTI EXTRAVAGANZA

We recently sponsored a successful Spaghetti Night. Everything was based on the noodle—from the meal to devotions.

Here are some of our activities:

Spaghetti Dinner. Start the event with the meal. You might consider awards for the sloppiest, the biggest eater, the neatest, etc. Give prizes of antacid, a bib, etc. (Don't serve up all the noodles! Save some for what follows.)

Pasta Pass. Have everyone draw an uncooked spaghetti noodle. Then, announce that the two people holding the shortest noodles are now team captains. They choose team members. Each member now takes a piece of uncooked spaghetti (which becomes a "pasta passer") and assembles in a line. The relay begins when the captain passes a piece of cooked spaghetti from his pasta passer to the next. The object is to pass the pasta down and back without using anything but the pasta passer. If a piece falls, the team must start over.

Noodle Knots. Divide into groups of four. Each team ties lengths of cooked spaghetti together, trying to make the longest continuous piece that can be held off the floor. Set a time limit. When time is called, the teams suspend their creations. The longest string wins. The losers eat their pieces.

Spaghetti Toes. Divide into two teams. Take off

shoes and socks. The object: to transport the most spaghetti by using only toes. Pass from person to person from a bowl to a plate at the other end. The team that transports the most in a given time is the winner.

Javelin Throw. Pick one person from each team to throw uncooked spaghetti the longest distance.

Spaghetti Coiffures. Each team dresses its captain with cooked spaghetti to resemble a hairdo. Arrange for pictures and judging.

Devotions. Following a couple of songs, a lesson on spaghetti will wrap up the whole evening. Using a cooked and uncooked piece of spaghetti, point out the need for the spaghetti to jump into the boiling water to find fulfillment. The same is true of the Christian: he must first lose his life to find it. The trials in our life build character and confidence in God, who supplies our needs. We are transformed as we discover new potential with God.

—Carl Heine, Kent, Washington

HUG TAG

Here's how to play this great crowd breaker. One person is "it." "It" tries to tag someone else—by hugging. There's no base—you're "safe" only when you are hugging someone else. Only two to a hug and you can't hug the same person two times in a row. You can hug for three seconds, then you must hug someone else. No tag-backs are allowed.

—Jill Hedlund, Belcourt, North Dakota

NO-GAS STOCK CAR RACE

Here's how your group can experience the thrills and spills of a stock car race, right in your church parking lot.

We took two old VW bugs (the older, the better) and had two teams. Each team was to paint its VW to look like a race car. We used water-based tempera paints. They are harmless to the finish and come off easily with soap and water. We used three different colors, but more could be used. We gave the teams a time limit and the best paint job won a prize.

Then we proceeded to have a stock car race. The only difference in this race was that the teams had to **push** their cars around an obstacle course. In order for everyone on the team to be used, we required that the car be filled with people (six at the most) while five or six members pushed. Then, as part of the race, the team had to hose down and wash all the paint off the cars.

It was a close race and everyone had a lot of fun.

—Audrey Saint, Lanham, Maryland

COLD KISS RELAY

Pucker up for some chewy fun with this game.

Divide your group into two teams. Appoint a sponsor to each team. On a "go" signal, give the first member on each team a peanut butter kiss. They are to chew it up and swallow it. Then the next team member gets a peanut butter kiss. The team that finishes first is the winner.

Now, here's the catch. Before you play the game, put your peanut butter kisses in the refrigerator long enough so that they become hard. Makes a very interesting chewing game!

—Barbara Milton, Rossville, Illinois

DON'T GET BURNED

Playing with matches is more fun than ever with "Don't Get Burned."

Using book matches (not kitchen matches), each person one-at-a-time reveals as many things about who he/she is before the match burns out (or burns a finger). Each item is worth one point. The youth leader keeps score. Here's an example: "My name is Harvey Ocra (1 point), I'm a junior at Millard Fillmore High (1 or 2 points), I play bassoon in the band (1 point), I have a toy poodle named Beast (1 point), I enjoy snorkeling (1 point), and I like vacations in Kansas (1 point)."

Each person goes on until he/she blows out the match or drops it. The winner is the one with the most points. Award a goofy prize to the winner (but not a book of matches—that's too predictable).

BODY CONNECTIONS

This is a takeoff on the old Twister game.

Prepare two pairs of dice. (You could use small square boxes or wooden blocks.) In each set you will have one die numbered 1 through 6, and on the other a diagram of six parts of the body: elbow, armpit, ear, knee, foot and nose.

Have teams of eight people, two to roll the dice and give the instructions, and six to follow the instructions. Each roller has one numbered die and one anatomy die. The other players are numbered from one to six. As the dice are tossed, the game begins.

One roller tosses a number 3 on the number die and a nose on the anatomy die. The other roller tosses number 6 on the number die and foot on the anatomy die. Now team member #3 must place his/her nose on team member #1's foot. They must hold this position throughout the game as well as comply with any further instructions given concerning their number, as it comes up on the toss of the dice.

This can be played with the idea of competition, how many different things can be accomplished before you fall or reach a physical impossibility, or merely as a crowdbreaker. We have found that it is extremely difficult to not become better acquainted with someone with whom you have just spent a few minutes being nose to nose or ear to armpit.

—Ken Blevens, Kerman, California

MYSTERY JIGSAW

We planned a "Howdy Party" for the beginning of the school year. But we needed a good way to attract attention to our kick-off gathering. So, we used a mystery jigsaw puzzle approach.

We bought a jigsaw puzzle and attached a piece of the puzzle to each invitation we mailed for our "Howdy Party." The invitations explained that the recipient was a unique part of our total program, as symbolized by the attached puzzle piece.

Each person was then asked to bring his/her piece of the puzzle to our meeting and find that special place where his/her part of the puzzle fit.

The puzzle idea worked well as an attention getter and it encouraged attendance. Plus, it served as an ice breaker as people arrived. People were welcomed and immediately became a part of the group as they tried to solve the mystery of where their piece fit best.

—Sylvan Knobloch, Charleston, Illinois

FRISBEE-SLIDING

Frisbee-sliding is a game that combines two of America's favorite pastimes—sliding and Frisbee-throwing. It gets everyone in your group involved and uses a minimal amount of equipment.

First, find a good slide in a park or elsewhere. Then, designate a member to throw the Frisbee.

The Frisbee-thrower tosses the Frisbee to members of the group as they come down separately. The member who catches three in a row gets to be the Frisbee-thrower and the game starts over. The Frisbee-catcher must not have his/her feet on the ground in any way when the Frisbee is caught.

This is a fun game, but there are many other ways to play it. For example, use two slides and two Frisbees and have half the group do relay races against the other half. The first team to complete its quota of caught Frisbees per person wins.

Slide a little slow? Going down backward will add some excitement.

—Kari Fisher, Austin, Minnesota

BEACH BALL FOOSBALL

Here's a game that can be called anything but boring. You will need a good-sized beach ball and a large room.

To play, divide the group into two teams. All of the members of one team sit in rows of three to five abreast, one row interspersed between the other team's rows, all team members facing the same direction. Each team

34

should have three to four rows.

Then, the other team sits with their backs to the team already seated.

If you're seated correctly, you should be glaring into the eyes of an opposing team member about two leg-lengths in front of you.

Every player must remain seated. Play and score just like regular foosball, a point for each time the beach ball goes over the opposing team's goalie row.

Variations include playing blindfolded, left hands only, and heads only.

—Duffy Robbins, Wilmore, Kentucky

COTTON FLAPJACKS

How are your flapjack skills? Find out with this crazy game.

You'll need two frying pans, two spatulas, two blind-folds and a box of cotton balls.

Choose two people to be blindfolded and seated on the floor. Give each a frying pan and spatula. Spread a couple dozen cotton balls in front of each contestant.

On a signal, each tries to flapjack the most cotton balls into his/her pan. The cotton balls must not be scooped up, only flapjacked.

The rest of the group may shout instructions to the contestants.

It's hilarious.

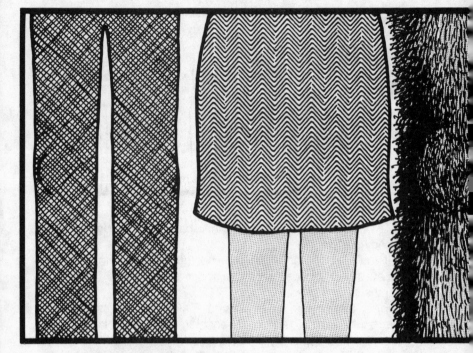

KNEE FEELERS

Here's a fun get-acquainted idea.

Take a person out of the room and blindfold him. At the same time, have five to eight people form a line facing the same way in the meeting room. The blindfolded person is brought back into the room and must guess the identities of the people in the line—by touching them from the knees down.

It is often difficult to guess correctly since everyone often wears similar pants and shoes to our meetings. We've had lots of fun with this game.

—Mike Utterback, Peoria, Illinois

TWINKLE-TWINKLE LITTLE TINSEL

We came up with a fantastic Christmas game. Get a box of tinsel. Divide the group into two-person teams and then give each team a piece of tinsel. The first partner holds the piece above the other's head. After the leader says "Go!" the first partner drops the piece of tinsel and it is the job of the other teammate to blow air at it, always keeping it above the floor while moving it across the room.

After the team crosses the room, the partners switch off and blow the piece of tinsel back to the starting point. Use of hands is not allowed.

It's an absolute riot watching everyone blowing these pieces of tinsel around the room.

—Ron Bodager, Newnan, Georgia

PENNY SOCCER

This is a great game that requires only a smooth floor and some small change. It's played like soccer, but uses a coin instead of a ball. It's hilarious to watch everyone run after a penny and try to kick it across the floor.

There are many variations to penny soccer. The best is to use coins of varying amounts. Keep score by allowing 25 points for a quarter, five points for a nickel, etc.

This is a good way to get everyone participating. You might even collect an offering with this game. Team members must supply the coins. The team with the most points wins. The "losing" team often digs out more money to keep the game going. All coins go into the offering.

—Mike Waers, Chesapeake, Virginia

WATERWORKS CHOIR

Our group is developing a choir that makes music in many different ways. But we don't use voices; we use musical water.

It takes some work and practice, but the results are worth it. The music sounds great. Here are some of our ideas:

1. Most people know about blowing across the top of a pop bottle to get a musical pitch. Tune the pitches by varying the level of water in the bottles (we tune to a piano). Varying the size of the bottles will also affect the pitch.

2. You'll also get musical notes by striking a bottle or jar that's partially filled with water. Use a spoon or knife as a mallet. Tuning is the same as #1.

3. We've added another unique sound by moistening a finger and running it around the edge of a crystal glass that's partially filled with water. Again, tuning is done by varying the level of water in the glass.

By tuning these "instruments" you can actually play music such as Christmas carols, hymns, or whatever. The Waterworks Choir is a lot of fun, involves teamwork, and creates a unique style of music.

—Eric Preibisius, San Diego, California

BALLOON STOMPERS

Find out who the stompers are in your group with this one.

Divide your group into two teams. Line up each team from shortest to tallest. Then count off. Each member blows up a balloon and ties it around his/her ankle with a piece of string.

Now your leader calls out a number. The two players with that number

come to the center of the room and try to stomp each other's balloon. If you stomp your opponent's balloon first, your team gets a point. Repeat this process until all have played. The team with the greatest number of points wins.

—Bruce Harris, Dover, Delaware

WINK 'N RUN

Try this one for a fun, fast-moving group game.

Seat all of your girls in a circle. Leave one chair open. Now a guy stands behind each chair. The guys put their hands behind their backs.

The object is for the guy standing behind the empty chair to get a girl into his chair. He does this by winking at one of the girls. That girl tries to run to his chair. The guy behind her chair tries to stop her by quickly putting his hands on her shoulders. If he's not fast enough, then he winks to try to lure a girl to his chair.

At this point, you may switch and put the guys in the chairs and let the girls do the winking.

—Carol Wain, Redondo Beach, California

VOLLEYCUP

Our group has come up with a game that is both fun and practical. To play volleycup all you need is: a few styrofoam cups, a table, and about six to 12 people. Divide up into two teams of equal size that sit at opposite sides of the table. One side starts out as the "serving side" (side A). Side B is the "receiving side." Side A serves one cup to the other side by simply hitting it with their hands. Side B will attempt to hit it back in the same manner.

The game continues until the cup is either hit off the table, missed or destroyed. Then Side B serves a new cup to Side A. The game can go on for any amount of time.

We have particularly enjoyed this game because few materials are required and it can be played for any amount of time.

—Jill Curfman, Volant, Pennsylvania

NAME GAME RHYTHM

Need to learn names fast? Here's a game that will help you get acquainted in a hurry.

Seat your group in a circle and choose a leader to start the game. Everyone begins by slapping his/her knees twice, followed by clapping hands twice, then snapping fingers—first the right, then the left. As the leader snaps his right fingers, he calls out his own name. Then, as he snaps his left fingers, he calls out the name of another player.

The rhythm continues as the person named by the preceding player calls out her own name and the name of another in the circle.

No player may call the name of the player who immediately preceded him. Any named player who stops the rhythm or fails to call a new name on the snap of the left fingers goes to the end of the circle (to the left of the leader). Meanwhile, all other players move one space to the right, filling the space vacated by the bumped player.

Here's the real catch. When you move to a new seat, you assume the name of the person who sat there at the beginning of the game. This really requires concentration and an effort to remember names.

The first person to move completely around the circle to his/her original starting point is the winner.

When you think you're really good, speed up the rhythm.

—Dick Fischer, Loveland, Colorado

AUTOGRAPH ROUNDUP

We used this fun game as a part of an overnight youth event.

Divide into groups of five or six, with a car and one adult per group. Each group then tries to obtain as many of the requested autographs as possible. This is not a race against time. It's a chance to meet new people.

No autograph can be used twice. Each group must stay together. The driver must observe and certify all signatures and additional details.

Here are autographs-to-find that we used:

1. A trucker or traveler who has traveled at least 50 miles today. Point of origination? Destination?

2. Any person (not in the group) who plans on going to church this weekend. Which church?

3. A person who is coming out of a bar. Name of bar?

4. A person who drives a big truck. What's his CB handle? What does he haul?

5. A person in your group who has talked to a radio announcer on duty tonight. Announcer's name?

6. A person who pumps gas. Name of station?

7. A cab driver. The most interesting passenger he's ever had?

8. Two who are out on a heavy date. What's the best part of their evening?

9. A check-out clerk who has sold you an orange. Place?

10. A person in your group who has observed, at close range, the "night life" of ducks or geese. Name of park or pond? Description of "night life"?

11. A person who has bowled a game over 140 tonight. Place?

If you wish, you could assign point values to the various autographs, and award a prize to the team with the greatest number of points.

—Jerry Wagoner, Rochester, Minnesota

PORKY-MALLOW

Here's a game that gets harder but funnier as you go along.

Divide your group into two or more teams. Give each player a toothpick and each team a marshmallow. The first player puts the marshmallow on his toothpick and then holds the toothpick with his teeth. You're now ready to start the game.

Pass the marshmallow from player to player by sticking your toothpick into the marshmallow and leaving it in as you pass it along. You are not allowed to use your hands. As the marshmallow is passed it accumulates one more toothpick from each player.

It's a riot to see the players trying to avoid being stuck by the other toothpicks already in the marshmallow.

The first team to finish is the winner. And the end product is a marshmallow that looks like a porcupine (porky-mallow).

—Ron Bodager, Newnan, Georgia

DISGUISED DINNER

This "crazy dinner" idea was a real success in our youth fellowship.

Upon arrival each youth was given a copy of our menu. It listed 16 strange-sounding items. Each was a secret code word for an actual dinner item. For example, "cholesterol push" was actually a roll and butter, and "butcher's special" was a knife. Then each diner was asked to fill in his/her menu with choices for each course of the meal. Everybody chose four different items for each course. There were four courses, so everyone eventually received 16 items.

The completed menus were collected by our adult sponsors, who then served the dinners to the kids—one course at a time. At the end of each course, all items were removed from the tables. We had four adults serving 16 youth.

This was a funny meal because the kids never knew what they were ordering. Some would unknowingly order their dessert first, and beans last. And some had to eat their baked potato with their fingers.

See the sample menu. Here's the secret key to the menu for your servers: 1—angel food cake, 2—corn, 3—knife, 4—mints, 5—potato, 6—toothpick, 7—fork, 8—raisins, 9—spoon, 10—carrots and celery, 11—chicken, 12—green beans, 13—cheese, 14—roll and butter, 15—punch, 16—napkin.

—Patricia DeFeo, Wilmington, Delaware

GROUP GROWTH GOODIES

2

BIBLE STUDY SCAVENGER

Here's a way to add a little action and a lot of objects to your Bible study.
This activity combines a Bible study, a scavenger hunt
and a "show-and-tell" session.

This unusual study be-
gins after you've completed
your planned Bible study.
Break into teams and divide
the passages you just studied among each team. (The
gospels and Old Testament
stories work best, but any
passage is okay if you think
hard enough.)

Now, using the passage
as a guide, list any item
that's mentioned or implied
in the passage. You'll have to use your imagination as
you reread the verse. Some possible objects aren't
always immediately obvious in the verses.

For instance, potential items from Mark 2:13-17 might
include water from the lake (verse 13); dusty footprints
from the crowd (verse 13); a tax receipt from the tax col-
lector's booth (verse 14); hamburger wrappers from the
dinner with the tax collectors and sinners (verse 15); cer-
tificates of achievement for the Pharisees who were law-
yers (verse 16); and a doctor's bill for the sick sinners
(verse 17).

Once each team has listed all the items in its passage, take an hour or so and scavenge the items from
around the church or neighborhood. At the end of the
time limit, one person on the team reads the passage
slowly while the remaining team members illustrate it
with the items.

After the scavenged study is over, you can use the

items in a "museum." Pick up some small tags from a business supply store or use 3x5 cards. Describe the item museum-style and list the Bible verse which mentions it.

Set up a creative display in an out-of-the-way area of the church and take church school classes on tours.

GARDEN OUTREACH

Our group tried an idea last summer that turned out great as a ministry and a fun project.

An elderly couple lives near our church. They were having problems with weeds taking over their backyard. In the past they'd kept a rather large vegetable garden, but were no longer able to maintain it because of health problems. So, our group asked for permission to clean up the yard and plant a new vegetable garden. We told the old folks they could keep any of the produce they wanted, and we'd give the rest to the shut-ins of our church.

The couple liked our idea. So we began planting and caring for the garden. We eventually harvested squash, cucumbers, carrots, eggplant, pumpkins and string beans.

Every Wednesday we piled ourselves and a load of vegetables into our church van and visited shut-ins. These sweet people really appreciated the fresh produce. But, even more than the food, they enjoyed the brief visits with our youth.

Whenever we'd have an oversupply of vegetables, we'd take them to the City Rescue Mission.

This project was successful not only to the shut-ins and the City Rescue Mission, but also to the elderly owners of the garden site. Our project gave them the joy of watching their garden being used and kept up, gave them something to look forward to, and filled their backyard with jovial young people with whom to talk and laugh. And the positive influence on our kids was greatly enriching too.

—Eric Preibisius, San Diego, California

DOMINO UNITY

Here's a good discussion starter on the subject of group unity.

As everyone enters, each person should take one domino. Hold on to it—it represents you. When everyone has arrived, create a design with the dominoes, with everyone putting his/her domino somewhere in the design. The dominoes should be placed on end and close enough to each other to make possible a chain reaction of knocking each other down should one of them be toppled over.

Members should take a moment to think about where they are going to put their dominoes in the design—near the center, on the end, or wherever.

After the design has been completed, members should answer in their own minds how they each fit into the design of the youth group.

After some discussion, someone should attempt to knock the dominoes down by gently pushing one of them over. See if they all fall down. If not, draw analogies of the importance of a closeness to each other in the group to make the group an effective body for Christ. If they all fall down, consider Hebrews 10:25—"Forsake not the assembling of yourselves together. . ."

Close with a challenge to invite friends to the group and imagine what kind of design could be made if 10 or 15 more kids were involved.

—David B. Ingram, Meridian, Mississippi

HEAVENLY PASS

Here's a thought-provoking exercise that can lead into a very interesting discussion.

Hand out 5" x 8" cards and pencils to the group members. Each person then writes a "pass" that might get him or her into heaven. The "pass" is an answer to the question, "If you were to die tonight, why should God let you into heaven?" Collect the cards and read some of them to the group. Then use the following questions for discussion:

1. How do you think someone who has never heard of Jesus Christ would answer the question?

2. Do you think someone who has never heard the gospel will be judged differently than someone who has? If so, what do you think the criteria for judgment might be?

3. Will our "good works" help us in any way when we face judgment? If so, in what way?

4. Is it possible for a person to know for certain that he or she will be admitted into heaven when he dies?

—David Taylor, Huntington Beach, California

IF I COULD

Here's a group sharing idea we've found successful. Everyone writes his/her name on a 3x5 card, folds it and drops it in a box. After stirring the cards, each person draws one from the box (pick another if his or her own name is drawn). Then, everyone reads the name on the card and gives that person an ''if I could'' gift, and tells why.

This activity can be a serious time or a fun time of gag gifts. Some of the kids in our group gave cars, new boy or girl friends, jobs, talents, success, love, friendship. We have seen some good times and a lot of participation with this simple activity.

—Rob Raynor, Newport News, Virginia

WHITE SHIRT PARTY

Here's a creative activity to help your members get to know one another better. It also works well in a retreat setting where·several groups gather together.

Round up old white dress shirts for everyone. You'll find them in your rag bags at home or at the Salvation Army and Goodwill stores. And you'll need a permanent ink felt-tip marker for each person. Spread some papers on the floor to protect it from the ink that may seep through the shirts.

50

Give these instructions to each person:

1. Write your first name on the front left pocket.
2. Write your last name under the back of the shirt collar.
3. On the back, write your favorite color and your height in centimeters.
4. Write your birthday.
5. Draw an animal you would like to be.
6. Answer: Why are you here?
7. Draw an eye the color of yours.
8. Identify your favorite musical instrument.
9. Draw a flower you like.
10. Write a nursery rhyme title.
11. List your hobbies.
12. Identify your favorite sport.
13. Write your favorite saying (words you like, a proverb, some philosophy, or a Bible verse).
14. Draw your favorite fruit.
15. What do you need to improve in yourself?
16. Identify a food you dislike.
17. Draw something that you like to do in the winter.
18. Draw your favorite possession.

When everyone is finished, each person should put on his shirt. Now continue with a mixer or your planned program for the evening. This is an easy and effective way to get acquainted. Suddenly all the people in the room are **wearing** their personalities where everyone can see them.

—Paul Freeman, Enid, Oklahoma

CARING RAID

It's a raid! Show your love for a needy family, an elderly couple, a lonely widow, or even an inactive group member by organizing a caring raid.

Arm the members of your raiding party with refreshments, song sheets and a Bible verse or two (2 Corinthians 13 is especially appropriate). Arrive unexpectedly, shouting, "We love you—this is a raid!" Spend some time feasting, singing and talking. Be sure not to leave a mess.

Your demonstration of love will be appreciated and long remembered.

—Shirley-Raye Redmond, Franklin, Illinois

PUBLICITY POSTERS

Here's a simple but effective way to publicize an upcoming group event.

Arouse curiosity by posting several large posters where they'll be well seen. Each poster should carry one of the following words (in big letters): WHAT? WHERE? WHO? HOW? WHEN? WHY? WHY NOT?

Leave these posters up for a week or so, then write in the details on each.

This method really draws attention and feeds upon people's natural curiosity.

—Kim Hall, Shreveport, Louisiana

PRAYER PROBE

For an overnight retreat in our church we used two different prayer exercises to go along with our theme on prayer.

The first one is "cliche prayers." Break up into small groups and have each group compose a prayer using all of the cliches they have ever heard used in prayers (everything from flowery introductions of God to overworked catch-all phrases). If your group is small you might want each member to compose a cliche prayer. Then share with the whole group. The results will not only be extremely entertaining, but very effective in pointing out what prayer should not be. You may take it a step further and trade cliche prayers, and then translate them to conversational type prayers. Then lead into a discussion on elements of effective prayer.

The second idea is "prayer bags." Supply each person with magazines and a brown lunch bag. Members then search through the magazines for pictures or words that represent the things they have recently prayed about. They can include things they have been thankful for as well as items they have asked for. Members snip the photos and words and put them in their bags. After everyone has finished have each person share his/her bag with the group, explaining how he/she has used prayer recently.

—Mrs. Linda K. Oliver, Albion, New York

PANTRY RAID

Here's a fun way to gather food for distribution to the needy. Organize a pantry raid.

Three weeks prior to our raid, we began announcements in Sunday morning church and in the church newsletter. The congregation was informed that our youth group would be coming around to "raid" everyone's pantries.

When "Raid Night" came, pairs of our members scattered to the homes of church members. At each house we asked the resident to rummage through the pantry to find some canned or boxed food to donate to the needy. One of the two youth handed out pamphlets explaining our purpose, while the other youth carried a box for collecting the food.

—Robert L. Beasley, Augusta, Georgia

CARNIVAL CAN NIGHT

Want a fun activity that will excite your youth group and help a local service organization? Try a Carnival Night. Carnival Night features several games: basketball shoot, ring toss, balloon bust, miniature golf, etc. Obtain some simple prizes to give away to the winners of the various games. Bubble gum, candy, and pens from local businesses make good prizes.

Here is the key to making your Carnival Night work. Each game requires a certain number of tickets. Tickets are obtained by trading canned goods. One canned good = 10 tickets. It's simple! The more canned goods you bring, the more you can play! The more you play, the more prizes you can win!

After your Carnival Night is over, donate the canned goods to a local service organization. That organization can provide food for needy families in your community.

—Doug Newhouse, Florence, Kentucky

SCRIPTURE HUNT

Want a new way for your group to search out the scriptures? Select a well-known Bible verse relating to the point of your meeting. Then write the first three words of the verse on a piece of paper. Continue till you finish the verse. Place the pieces of paper around various spots in your meeting area.

Group members must find the papers and organize them into the correct order. After juggling the papers into correct order, discuss the meaning of the verse.

—Dennis and Susan Henn, Wenatchee, Washington

MAP FOR LOST MEMBERS

Try this one on any of your members who have dropped out of activities.

Send the inactive member a personalized map, showing how to get to the church from his/her house. Add all sorts of funny or interesting details on the route. Include a note explaining that you assumed that the missing member had forgotten how to get to the church.

Also add a sincere note that you really do miss them and you'd like to see them active again.

—David R. Helms, Rossville, Georgia

THE BODY EATS BREAKFAST

Here's a crazy variation of a skit that will get lots of laughs and also illustrate 1 Corinthians 12:12-30.

Divide your group into teams of six. Have each of the six team members become one of the following body parts:

"Eyes"—this person is the only one in the group who isn't blindfolded. While "eyes" can't use his arms or talk, he can whisper to "mouth" and listen to "ears."

"Ears"—blindfolded and can't use his arms or talk,

56

can only whisper with "mouth" and "eyes."

"Mouth"—blindfolded, can't use arms, repeats only what "ears" tells him.

"Right arm"—blindfolded, uses right arm only upon commands from "mouth."

"Left arm"—blindfolded, uses left arm only upon commands from "mouth."

"Legs"—blindfolded, stands on hands and knees between "mouth's" legs, moves forward, backward, left or right only on "mouth's" commands.

The "right arm," "ears," and "left arm" lock arms. "Mouth" stands behind "ears" and hangs on to "ears'" waist.

Ahead of time, prepare a bowl of shredded wheat and water for each team. Make sure the concoction is super messy before starting the contest. Place the bowls 15-20 feet from the "body." (You could also have the body brush "mouth's" teeth.)

The object of the activity is for the "body" to move to the bowl of cereal, pick it up, eat the cereal and return to the starting place. Remember "legs"? He's on his hands and knees under "mouth's" mouth. He'll probably get his head and shoulders plastered with soggy shredded wheat.

Here's a sample of the action: "Eyes" tells "ears" to tell "mouth" to move forward. "Mouth" tells the rest of the body to move forward. "Eyes" tells "ears" to turn right or left and to stop. The going can get hilarious when "eyes" tells "ears" to tell "mouth" to tell "right arm" and "left arm" to start feeding "mouth." (One arm holds the bowl while the other arm spoons the food toward "mouth."

The rules are simple. The body parts can only perform those functions specifically assigned to them. If the "body" breaks apart or starts talking with other parts, the whole "body" has to start from the beginning again.

After the "body" has eaten, you can discuss how each body part felt about being such a small part of the body. Read 1 Corinthians 12:12-30. Discuss practical applications this passage has for the youth group and for the entire church.

STAND ON NUMBERS

This is a "strength of feeling" exercise.

Pass out paper and pencils. Each member copies a list of issues such as abortion, politics, school, feminism, censorship, church, police, soap operas, names of singers or television shows. Each chooses a number between one and seven that indicates how he or she feels toward each issue. "One" indicates strongly negative feelings, "seven" indicates strongly positive feelings.

While members work on this, the leader places sheets marked one through seven on the floor in a straight line, about two feet apart.

After members finish ranking each issue, the leader asks them to stand on the number corresponding to the first issue. They stand there only a few seconds, looking around the room and seeing where the group stands. Then the leader calls the second issue, and so on.

This is a good method to kick off a discussion on any topic.

—Glenn Davis, Winston-Salem, North Carolina

PEOPLE COLLAGES

"People Collages" will help you see how others see you, and it's a lot of fun, too.

You'll need a pile of old magazines and enough paste, scissors and sheets of construction paper for every member.

Begin by placing each person's name in a hat. Then everyone draws a name (be sure you don't draw your own name). Don't let others see the name you have drawn.

Now create a collage that depicts the person whose name you've drawn. Find appropriate pictures and words in the magazines and paste them in an artistic way on the construction paper.

When everyone's finished, each person steps to the front of the room to display his collage. See if the group can guess who is depicted in each collage.

You might conclude with a discussion on "how others see us."

—Lois Silvey, Alexandria, Pennsylvania

MORE HAMBURGER THAN STEAK

This is a fun exercise to help everyone get acquainted.

The leader asks participants to think whether they are more to one extreme or another. For example, the leader asks: "Are you more hamburger than steak?" Those who are more like "steak" go to the opposite side of the room. Participants pair off and discuss briefly why they are more "hamburger" or "steak."

Repeat the exercise by naming other extremes.

Here's a list we've used: country/city, TV/books, leader/follower, pioneer/settler, giver/receiver, breakfast/dinner, spectator/participant, early-riser/late-nighter, mountains/beach, tiger/kitty cat, clown/straight man, country-western/classical, Cadillac/Datsun, spender/saver.

—Glenn Davis, Winston-Salem, North Carolina

THE MUSIC BOX

We have found a monthly Christian album giveaway to be a welcome addition to our youth program.

We fixed up a locking metal box with a slot in the top and a sign that said "The Music Box." At each youth group activity, members may sign a slip of paper and drop it into the box. At the last activity of the month, the winning name is drawn from the box. The winner must be present to claim the album.

"The Music Box" accomplishes two objectives: better attendance, and promotion of Christian music.

—Andy Robertson, Hueytown, Alabama

MEETING IN THE DARK

Here's a meeting idea to illustrate Jesus as the light of the world.

Have your regular program in a totally darkened room. Start with songs, a game, announcements and refreshments (popcorn). End with a devotion.

To start the devotion, light a small candle. After about 45 minutes in the dark, the light should be a relief to the group. Discuss: Survey the chaos around you (popcorn, especially). How was the darkness? Was it easy to work together? Who got refreshments and who didn't? Did we trust each other in the dark? Compare Christ's light in a confused world to the candle light in the devotion.

Pass out candles to everyone. Then pass the light around.

—Richard Davis, Lewisville, Texas

PHOTO TEAMS

Stop and think about the kinds of things your group could do if you could equip small teams with a camera for around $5 a team.

The people at Workshop for Learning Things, 5 Bridge St., Waterton, MA 02172, sell a plastic camera with a flash attachment for $5. The phone number is (617) 926-1160. Check on available quantities and current prices before ordering. The cameras take regular film, so any supermarket or drugstore can keep you well supplied.

The cameras aren't completely automatic, so you'll have to get someone to explain how the simple shutter and aperture settings work.

Once each team has a camera, the only limitation is its ability to be imaginative and creative.

Here are some ideas to get you started into the world of youth group photography.

• Illustrate a passage of scripture using photos.
• Create a cartoon strip type story where photos replace the cartoons. Write captions to tell the story.
• Develop a story book for young children by using photos instead of artwork. Print the story in large letters.
• Illustrate a specific theme you'll be studying.
• Photograph everyone's eyes (or noses or ears or knees or feet) and make a creative poster to publicize your group at church.
• Using a balcony as a platform, photograph a message that's written below. People spell out the words by using their bodies to form letters.
• Have people in the team photograph things that tell others about themselves (hobbies, interests, likes, dislikes, etc.).
• Have a photo scavenger hunt. Each team tries to photograph all items on a list.

HOW WELL DO YOU KNOW ME?

This game shows how well friends know each other. Divide into pairs. One person leaves the room and the other sits in a chair facing the group. The person in the chair receives seven or eight pieces of paper and a pen. The leader asks him/her about the person absent from the room. Examples:
• "What piece of your friend's clothing do you like best?"
• "What is your friend's favorite color, food, animal?"
• "What do you two discuss a lot?"
The person in the chair writes the answers to each question on a sheet of paper. After the questions have been answered, the other friend comes back into the room and stands behind the person in the chair. The leader repeats the questions to the newcomer. If the friends' answers differ, the leader blows an obnoxious horn. If the answers match, the pair wins 10 points. The friends then change roles and repeat the game.

The pair with the greatest number of points wins the game.

—Karen Hartman, Prince George, British Columbia

LOVE SONGS

Want to get inactive members back in the youth group? Try adding this ingredient to your next youth visitation adventure to homes of your inactives. This is especially fun around Christmas.

Have the whole group go "caroling" together. Use tunes of favorite Christmas carols and add new lyrics. The carol might go something like this:

We missed you on Sunday morning,
We missed you on Sunday morning,
We missed you on Sunday morning and Sunday
* night too.*
Good tidings we bring of our next youth fling,
Good tidings from Christians who really do care!

(Sung to the tune of "We Wish You a Merry Christmas.")

Why not raid the refrigerator while you talk to the inactive member about upcoming youth events?

—David R. Helms, Rossville, Georgia

FUN
FUND
RAISERS

THE DIME-A-DIP DINNER

Want to change the standard boring fellowship dinner into a simple fund raiser? How about a "Dime-a-Dip Dinner"?

Two weeks prior to the event, our group called members of the congregation and asked them to bring various meats, vegetables, salads and desserts for the "dip" dinner.

At the dinner itself, the folks paid a dime per dip of food that they chose. They were surprised and delighted that they received a super meal for a small cost, and it was an easy way to earn between $150 and $200.

Make sure the dinner is well-publicized and provide some entertainment.

—Michele Grove, Hampstead, Maryland

AUCTION SNACKS

A steady year-round way to make money for your group is a refreshment service at auctions.

We contacted a local auctioneer and expressed our willingness to provide refreshments at all of his auctions. He liked the idea. We provide the table, coffee pots and other equipment. We keep the menu simple—coffee, Kool-Aid, doughnuts and hot dogs.

Several times during each auction, the auctioneer encourages the crowd to visit our stand. We earn $60 to $100 per day. And we need only three or four people to run the stand.

—Mary Allen, Austin, Minnesota

CHRISTMAS LUMINARIA SALE

Luminarias are traditionally lighted in the Southwest on Christmas Eve to signify lighting a path for the Wise Men. These little lanterns made from paper sacks are placed along the edges of sidewalks and driveways.

Our group made and sold luminarias for $2.50 per dozen. All you need are paper sacks (No. 3 size), sand and votive candles. We found sand free for the digging, sacks at $5 per thousand and candles at $1.29 for 36.

Luminarias can be made in an assembly line process. Fold down the top two inches of the bag. This adds stability. Then pour in about an inch of sand and place the candle in the center.

When delivering luminarias to customers, place them about three feet apart along the edges of the sidewalks. You can use small torches or railroad flares to light the candles.

We sold 70 dozen luminarias. We also set up 300 luminarias around our church on Christmas Eve.
—Clo Mingo, Los Alamos, New Mexico

FERTILIZER SALE

Need a good springtime fund raiser? Sell fertilizer! It's one of those products many people need to buy, and they might as well help green their lawns and your group's treasury at the same time.

We publicized our fertilizer sale and took orders at church for several Sundays. We also spent a couple Saturdays selling door to door. Our members were given careful information about the fertilizer's chemical content, so that they could answer any questions.

After collecting all our orders, we bought the 50-pound bags of fertilizer from a local fertilizer company. They delivered the stuff to the church on a designated Saturday. Customers then came and presented their receipts to claim their fertilizer.

We raised over $1,900 on this project.
—Jan Hancock, Dallas, Texas

HUNGER KIDNAP

Kidnap your minister and help fight world hunger at the same time.

Our youth group kidnapped our pastor on a Saturday night and held him for ransom. While he was tied and blindfolded, our members called each family in the congregation. We requested a ransom of money and/or canned goods, to be brought to church the next morning to help fight hunger.

After we placed all the calls, we had a lock-in and studied the problems of world hunger and prepared a worship service for the following morning.

We collected $115 and 95 canned goods. The money was sent to World Vision and the food was given to needy families in our area.

—Lynndel Messmore, Galesburg, Illinois

PARENTS' DAY OUT

To raise money for the annual UNICEF campaign, we organized a Saturday Parents' Day Out, when our group cared for church members' children while mom and dad went Christmas shopping.

Scheduled for the first Saturday in December, we advertised the Parents' Day Out in our church newsletter and Sunday bulletins. We asked people to sign up and include their children's names, ages, arrival and departure times, and any special instructions such as nap time or eating habits.

Our list of customers was too short when our cut-off date arrived, so we decided to use the church directory and contact all parents with small children. After this we ended up with 25 kids.

Our group members staffed the day from 9 a.m. to 4 p.m., working in two-hour shifts. We divided the kiddies into age groupings, and assigned some of our members to each grouping. We showed cartoons and movies continuously throughout the day. Other indoor and outdoor activities were also provided.

We furnished apple juice and cookies to our young customers. Children with us over the lunch hour brought a sack lunch.

Our only expenses were rental fees for the movies (25 cents each from the public library) and the cost of the apple juice. Cookies were donated by group members. We charged $1.25 per hour for a family's first child, and 75 cents per hour for each additional child in a family. We profited $65.

And, some of our members were able to line up future babysitting jobs through our Parents' Day Out.

—Ginny Howard, Winston-Salem, North Carolina

BAKE-IN

When our group was a little short on funds we decided to cook up a little cash with a "bake-in" fund raiser. A bake-in is like a bake sale, but instead of baking alone at home, everyone comes to the church kitchen on a Saturday and bakes together.

We met on Saturday morning with our recipes. We figured out quantities needed for each ingredient and then went shopping together. We provided our own cooking utensils.

We sold our baked-in goods the next day after the morning worship service. Everything sold quickly. We enjoyed working together and having a chance to show off our culinary talents. And the congregation loved having goodies to munch on after church.

—Kari Fisher, Pueblo, Colorado

ROCK CONCERT

Get your group together this spring and throw some rocks. And get paid for it.

Our group clears farmers' fields of stones before the spring planting. The farmers appreciate our service. They're happy to pay us because our rock-clearing service saves them the expense of repairing rock-damaged machinery later in the season.

The farmers furnish the tractor, wagon and driver. They pay either by the acre or by the total hours worked. We've made as much as $75 in two hours with a group of eight or ten.

The fellowship and exercise are great, especially while unloading the rocks. All the noise produced by the rocks hitting each other inspired our nickname for this fund raiser—rock concert.

Mr. and Mrs. Dale Myers, St. Johns, Michigan

CARHOP COOKOUT

The fund raising dinner is a reliable old idea. But we've found a new twist—a drive-in dinner.

We have a big parking lot where people can drive in and place their orders for hot dogs and hamburgers. They choose their fare from our hamburger-shaped menus. Our members grill the hamburgers and hot dogs outside. Another crew puts on the fixin's in the kitchen.

Some of our girls dress up in carhop outfits—pigtails

and all—and roll up to the customers' cars on roller skates.

Fifties music is blaring in the parking lot to set the right atmosphere.

Creative names for our sandwiches add to the fun—Wimpburger (plain), Breathburger (with onions), Lonely Dog (plain), etc.

Each member brings something to donate, such as four bags of chips or two pounds of hamburger. So, all the money we take in is profit.

We've easily made over $100 both times we've tried this idea.

Gary Moran, Albemarle, North Carolina

COLLECTIVE AUCTION

We raise funds in a fun and lucrative way. First of all, contributions of objects (books, records, etc.) are received. Then each item is auctioned, but not in the usual way.

A judge sets an alarm to go off at an unknown, pre-arranged time (one minute, 30 seconds, two minutes or whatever). All may bid as much as they want, regardless of how much was previously bid. When the alarm goes off, the item goes to the last bidder. Now, **all** bids are collected.

For example: Fred bids, "One dollar!" Janet bids, "Two fifty!" Harold bids, "Two dollars!" Ring! Harold wins the item and $5.50 is collected.

—Bruce Filson, Montreal, Quebec

CHRISTIAN SKATE

Every sixth Wednesday we sponsor an evening of Christian roller skating. And we net more than $100 profit each time.

We rent a local rink from 8:30 to 11 p.m. We use our own DJs and contemporary Christian music. Admission is $2. Attendance averages 200.

We draw kids from all kinds of churches. And we hardly have to advertise anymore—just a few posters here and there.

David Wiebe, Winnipeg, Manitoba, Canada

MAKE ME LAUGH

For fun and profit, our group put on a "Make Me Laugh" show.

We bought $30 worth of props (disguises, costumes, etc.) and prepared a bunch of funny jokes and gags. We publicized the show and invited the congregation. Each person who thought he/she could keep a straight face was asked to put up a minimum of $1. If we made him/her laugh, we got to keep the money. If we couldn't provoke laughter, the contestant's money was returned.

Our group members then let loose with their funny stuff. One member did an Ernest Angely impersonation and "cured" somebody of an ear problem by pulling cauliflowers from his ears. Another boy dressed up as "The Hulk"—green paint and all. Someone else read funny news headlines. Another one did a routine as "Diaper Man."

As it turned out, everybody laughed, and we kept all the money—more than $100. Some of our profits came from selling hot dogs and soda afterwards.

Everyone had a great time. Next we're going to try a "$1.98 Beauty Contest."

—Carrell Stokes, St. Peters, Missouri

SUPER BOWL SUB SUNDAY

Here's a fun fund raiser based on Americans' addiction to the Super Bowl.

"Super Bowl Sub Sunday" allows everyone to stay out of the kitchen and in front of the TV. Our members delivered submarine sandwiches to homes on Super Bowl Sunday.

We have only eight members in our group, but this project was very successful. Starting a month before the Super Bowl, we advertised our sub sandwich sale. We announced the sale in church, and sold door-to-door. We promised that we would deliver the subs before the game started, so that no one needed to worry about cooking on the big day.

We charged $3 for a whole sub, and $1.50 for a half sub. We used 15-inch rolls and put 4 slices of cheese, hard salami, boiled ham and bologna in each sandwich. We used a food processor to slice tomatoes, lettuce and onions that were added to the subs. Commercial Italian salad dressing was sprinkled on each sandwich. The subs were then wrapped in foil.

We sold 170 subs and made $230 profit. We've decided to make this an annual event.

—Senior Youth Group, United Presbyterian Church, Flanders, New Jersey

CONGREGATIONAL CHRISTMAS CARD

Writing and mailing stacks of Christmas cards can be tedious. Well, our group came up with an energy-saving idea. We made a huge Christmas card, using poster board, felt, glitter and paint. We patterned it off a regular card. We placed our supercard near the front door of the church.

A sign near the card instructed church members to send Christmas tidings to their church friends by simply jotting their greetings on the big card. They were urged to then donate the cost of cards and postage to the youth group.

Publicity was generated in our Sunday bulletin, church newsletter and during Sunday announcements.

The cost for materials was less than $5. We profited $200 on the project.

—Renee Lofgren, Peoria, Illinois

71

TURKEY TASTE TESTERS

Our group sponsored a fund raiser last year which has turned into an annual event because of the great response.

This is held the Sunday after Thanksgiving. We encouraged the congregation to bring favorite desserts and turkey dishes. There were five categories for the contestants: 15-year-old and under, men only, gourmet, quick 'n easy, and mom's home cookin'. We put out the dishes after the morning worship and charged $1 per item for non-entrants, 25¢ for entrants. Since it was a contest, we gave each person 10 pennies to vote with. Cups were put beside each dish for votes. We encouraged "cheating" by asking people to stuff the ballot cup with change from pockets and purses. Winners were those with the most change in the cups. They received ribbons and were reported in the church newsletter.

The youth group provided drinks, paper plates and forks. We placed chairs in the room but no tables to encourage people to mingle and keep sampling. We also sold copies of the recipes for 10¢ each. The group made over $125 and everybody seemed to enjoy the contest.

—Sharon Gregg, Mt. Prospect, Illinois

CHRISTMAS TREE DISPOSERS

Here's a worthwhile service and a good fund raiser. Offer a Christmas tree disposal service.

Before Christmas advertise your service of visiting customers' homes and carefully removing their Christmas

trees. Take orders and set up a schedule.

Take an old sheet or bedspread so you can wrap up the dead tree before moving it. This minimizes scattering needles all over the floor.

Once outside you can chop of the limbs and put them in a plastic bag, ready for trash pick up. You can also chop the remaining trunk into two-foot lengths, bundle them up, and sell them for firewood.

Some groups charge $5 for the tree disposal service. Some do it for free, collecting pledges from others for each tree serviced.

—Ruby MacDonald, Vancouver, Washington

HOT POTATO SALE

With the opening of restaurants with baked potato specialties in Dallas, our group cashed in on the craze by hosting a potato feast for the congregation after Sunday worship.

The Saturday before the luncheon our group met at the church kitchen to bake the potatoes and prepare salads and toppings for the potatoes. The toppings we offered were butter, sour cream, cheese, bacon bits and chili.

Sunday morning we heated the potatoes during worship. After the benediction we quickly set up for the potato feast. We charged $2 ($1.25 for children) for a potato, salad and drink. We also sold baked goods each of us brought from home. We raised over $160 and provided the congregation a nutritious and light meal.

—Julie Clapp, Dallas, Texas

JUNK METAL COLLECTION

To earn $3,000 for a mission trip to an orphanage in Mexico, we used many fund raisers. The most successful of these was recycling scrap metal.

After calling some scrap metal dealers, we found there is quite a market. We collected everything containing metal: water heaters, motors, refrigerators, car parts, aluminum cans, pipes, you name it. We publicized our project in our congregation and began getting several calls for pick-up. We also looked along roads and in old dumping sites. We even stopped at homes and businesses where we saw scrap lying around and found most folks eager to get rid of it.

After we had a full load we returned to the church and disassembled it all, separating the metals. We also collected lead, car batteries and insulated wire. We needed only a couple of complete tool boxes, several magnets and a vehicle. One of the generous men of the church loaned us his flatbed truck on Saturdays and paid for all the gas.

Everyone who planned to go on the Mexico trip was required to work. All 20 of the kids became true "junkers." We had great fun taking all those motors, furnaces, lawn mowers and appliances apart. We also felt good about cleaning up our community and recycling nonrenewable resources.

In just four months our group recycled what would have been junk into over $1,500.

—Marc Trueb, Oregon City, Oregon

74

SURPRISE WINDSHIELD WASH

The church members parked their cars and gathered inside for Mass as usual. They were oblivious to the sneak attack about to be launched on their car windows.

The youth group, armed with spray bottles of window cleaner and rags, washed all of the church members' car windows while Mass was in session. Then, just before the worshippers were dismissed, one of the youth announced that all of the car windows in the church parking lot had been washed by the group. It was explained that the youth were at the doors of the church with baskets to receive donations for the window washing service. The congregation was told exactly how the money was to be used. The congregation was dismissed and money began pouring into the baskets. (We gently rang a bell to remind those who may have forgotten the announcement.)

The response was overwhelming, almost $1 per donation! We had anticipated a $60 profit but ended with $170. Expenses were minimal. Each young person was responsible for bringing rags and a spray bottle of window cleaner. We made sure we had a gallon of cleaner for refill.

Besides making a profit, our group had a good experience working together. The church members were proud of the group's useful and clever effort. Remember, there should be no advance notice! Surprise is a big part of the fund raiser's success.

—Carter Lyons, Harrisonburg, Virginia

HOMEMADE TAKE-HOME TV DINNER SALE

Here is an idea for your group to raise funds and provide a meal for people in the congregation who want to watch a Sunday televised event (such as a football game) beginning at noon, just as the morning worship service is concluding.

Our youth prepared casserole dishes and packaged them in disposable containers (with salad and dessert). Then they sold them in a high visibility area to folks as they left for home after worship.

During the Sunday prior to the sale, we announced the upcoming fund raiser, emphasizing that the dinners would help the youth and lift some of the pressures facing the church members. (Members won't have to worry about going out to eat, can get home to watch most of the game, and won't need to prepare something before coming to church.) It was further publicized in the morning bulletin and the church newsletter. "Feed your faces and fund the fun-loving youth of the church" was a good slogan.

We sold the dinners at a minimum price but allowed for generous donations in order not to undersell our product. As a result, with just 10 participants, we raised $350 toward our winter retreat.

—Charles Stewart, Missouri City, Texas

LIVE MANNEQUINS

Our group became "live dummies" at a local department store. Working through the promotion director of the store, the young people selected two or three outfits of clothing from the racks. On a rotating basis, the youth posed as live mannequins in four or five staging areas, including the display windows. They were not allowed to move for a period of approximately 10 to 15 minutes. Once a model moved, smiled or laughed, the modeling session at that area was over. It's quite a challenge to keep a straight face when your friends stand outside the windows and make faces!

The store did not give the group any money. Their contribution was providing the clothing and the modeling areas. Our youth raised money by soliciting pledges for each minute they actually posed in immobile positions. They posed two or three times, wearing a different outfit each time. Even at 5 cents per minute, the money added up. The average was $45 in pledges per youth. (One girl earned over $90.)

The store can receive a great deal of attention—from customers and the media—with this project. So, many stores may be willing to pay your group a set amount.

The kids had a great time. Customers actually came up to them without realizing they were alive. They fingered and discussed the clothing. When they finally realized the mannequin was alive, the reactions were hilarious.

—John W. Baker, Rolla, Missouri

SINGING VALENTINES

Just before Valentine's Day our group offered "singing valentines." Customers would pay us to call their sweethearts and sing them a love song.

Here's how it worked. A few weeks before Valentine's Day we spread the word about our "singing valentine" service. We put notices in the church newsletter, and we put up posters in the high school. We kept our "singing valentine" fee small so that anyone could order at least one. We charged 50 cents per call. When taking orders, we asked for the sweetheart's name and phone number, and the name of a song to be sung to the sweetheart. (We offered a list of possible songs, such as "You Are My Sunshine" and "Happy Valentine's" sung to the tune of "Happy Birthday.")

Then, on the night before Valentine's Day, our group split up into teams of six or seven and went to different homes for the calling. (An office building with several phones would have worked better.) Our teams then made the calls, explaining first to the sweethearts that these special "singing valentines" were sent by so-and-so.

We made 110 calls, earning $55. And we received requests to continue the service for birthdays and anniversaries.

Susan E. Norman, Kernersville, North Carolina

ALL-CHURCH BAKE-OFF

The All-Church Bake-Off is a delicious fund raiser that can involve everyone in your congregation. We raised $2,500 the first year and $4,000 the second year.

Church members are all encouraged to enter the Bake-Off by submitting baked goods in any of five categories—cakes, pies, cookies, candies and breads. First-place winners in each category receive trophies. Other top winners receive ribbons.

After the judging, the baked goods are auctioned. By this time, the Bake-Off has attracted so much attention that auction attendance is great and bids are high.

Here are our rules for the Bake-Off: 1) No age limit. 2) Enter as many items as you wish in any or all of the five categories. 3) Entries must be in by noon on the Sunday of the Bake-Off. 4) Entries become the property of the youth group so that they can be sold at auction.

Our judges (one per category) are selected from outside the church. We try to find caterers, bakers and other professionals. Judges are asked to meet in our fellowship hall at 2 p.m. They score each entry—giving first consideration to taste. Appearance is secondary. After a top winner in each category is established, all judges taste these and vote on a grand prize winner.

After the evening service that night, everyone converges on the fellowship hall for the announcement of winners and the giant auction. We don't have a professional auctioneer in our congregation, so we use a good P.R. person to do the auctioneering.

We encourage everyone to enter. It's not just the grandmas who have kitchen talents. Matter of fact, a 15-year-old male athlete once won the grand prize.

To help promote the Bake-Off we encourage entrants to publicly challenge other people in the congregation. We publish about 25 persons' challenges in the church bulletin—"Mary Guest challenges Bob Galley," etc. Those challenged do not have to accept, but the bulletin puts them on the spot, and they usually participate.

We're also planning to gather the prize-winning recipes and sell a special cook book.

—Charles Stewart, Houston, Texas

NOTE

Got a winning youth group idea? GROUP Magazine constantly hunts for creative and fresh youth group crowd breakers, games, parties, worships, fund raisers, retreats and special events.

If your group has a good idea, please share it with thousands of other youth groups in the "Try This One" feature in GROUP. Your idea may be exactly what others have been hunting for to use in their own groups. Send your ideas to:

"Try This One"
GROUP Magazine
P.O. Box 481
Loveland, CO 80539

You'll get a check for each idea published.

OTHER YOUTH MINISTRY BOOKS FROM GROUP BOOKS:

The Basic Encyclopedia for Youth Ministry—Answers, ideas, encouragement, and inspiration for 230 youth ministry questions and problems. By Dennis C. Benson and Bill Wolfe. Hardbound. $15.95.

The Youth Group How-to Book—Detailed instructions and models for 66 practical projects and programs to help you build a better group. $14.95.

Youth Group Travel Directory—A nationwide listing of churches that will offer lodging and fellowship to your group at little or no cost. $7.95.

The Best of Try This One—A fun collection of games, crowd breakers and programs. $5.95.

More . . . Try This One—More games, fund raisers, crowd breakers, discussions and projects. $5.95.

_____The Basic Encyclopedia for Youth Ministry. $15.95.
_____The Youth Group How-to Book. $14.95.
_____Youth Group Travel Directory. $7.95.
_____The Best of Try This One. $5.95.
_____More . . . Try This One. $5.95.
_____Try This One . . . Too. $5.95.

Subtotal	$	_____
Postage and handling	$	2.00
Total enclosed	$	_____

NAME_____

ADDRESS _____

CITY_____STATE_____ZIP_____

SEND TO: **Group Books, Box 481, Loveland, CO 80539**